LOVE & DEVOTION

A SPOUSE'S MEMOIR

BOUND BY OUR VOWS

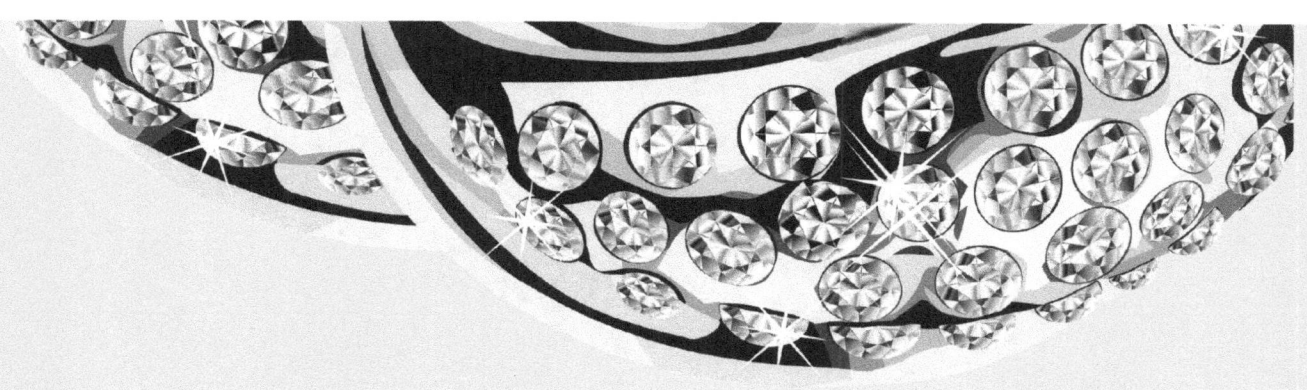

Atosha Logan

LOVE & DEVOTION

A SPOUSE'S MEMOIR
BOUND BY OUR VOWS

Atosha Logan

FOR PERMISSION REQUESTS, CONTACT THE AUTHOR AT:
ATOSHA LOGAN, AUTHOR & PUBLISHER
INFO@ATOSHALOGAN.COM
WWW.ATOSHALOGAN.COM

ISBN: 979-8-9931753-0-0 (PAPERBACK) 979-8-9931753-1-7 (E-BOOK)
FIRST EDITION

PRINTED IN THE UNITED STATES OF AMERICA

COVER DESIGN: ATOSHA LOGAN
INTERIOR LAYOUT: ATOSHA LOGAN

About the Author

Atosha Logan is a woman of faith, strength, and purpose who has dedicated more than two decades to the field of education and is an author, life coach, and consultant. Guided by her unwavering belief in God, she has poured her heart into nurturing, mentoring, and leading others with integrity and personal motivation. Her journey reflects resilience, hope, and a deep commitment to uplifting and empowering others.

Beyond her professional calling, Atosha treasures the bonds of family and the importance of legacy. She believes that life's experiences are not only meant to be lived but also shared as testimonies of God's grace. Her passion for legacy and storytelling is rooted in a belief that God's grace carries us through every season. This memoir is her gift of love, hope, and inspiration for generations to come.

She continues to live out her purpose with faith at the center, striving to leave behind a legacy of inspiration, love, and unwavering trust in God.

info@atoshalogan.com
www.atoshalogan.com

ACKNOWLEDGEMENTS

This memoir is the reflection of many hearts and hands that have touched my life, and I am deeply grateful for each one.

God has BLESSED me with a wonderful husband and three children.

To my family—you are my foundation and my greatest source of love and support. Thank you for standing beside me through every season of joy and trial, and for reminding me daily of the meaning of unconditional love. I am grateful for the wisdom you've shared and the lessons that continue to guide my journey. Each of you has left an imprint on my story that cannot be erased.

To my close friends, thank you for your laughter, encouragement, and honesty. Your presence has been a light in both the brightest and darkest moments, and your belief in me gave me the courage to keep writing.

Most of all, I give thanks to God. Without His grace, strength, and faithfulness, none of this would have been possible. Every chapter of my life is a testament to His unfailing love.

The Legacy of Jerald & Willie Mae Williams shall continue through me!
A Legacy to Live For Inc.

This

Spouse's Memoir

belongs to:

_____

DATE:

A Spouse's Memoir of Love & Devotion

A Spouse's Memoir
Introduction

Love, in its truest form, is a journey of partnership—weathering storms, celebrating milestones, and cherishing quiet moments in between. This memoir is a testament to the bond of two lives intertwined. With tenderness and truth, it honors the beauty of commitment, the strength of unity, and the lasting legacy of shared love.

From the roots that anchor us to the branches that stretch toward new horizons, these pages capture both struggle and victory. Each memory serves as a reminder that while we cannot control every circumstance, we can shape the legacy we leave behind.

This memoir is more than a story—it's an invitation to reflect on your own journey, to honor the memories that shape you, and to be inspired to live with courage and hope. reminding you of where you've been, who has walked beside you, and the dreams still waiting ahead.

Open these pages, take part in the journey, and let it spark reflection, conversation, and connection in your own life with grace, gratitude, and courage.

A SPOUSE'S MEMOIR
Table of Content

A SPOUSE'S MEMOIR OF LOVE & DEVOTION

"BE YOURSELF; EVERYONE ELSE IS ALREADY TAKEN."
— OSCAR WILDE

A SPOUSE'S MEMOIR OF LOVE & DEVOTION

All About
ME

FULL NAME :

NICKNAME

DATE OF BIRTH

LOCATION

HOSPITAL

MOTHER

FATHER

FAVORITE COLOR(S)

PERSONALITY

WEIGHT AT BIRTH

HOME ADDRESS

PHONE NUMBER

SIBLINGS

FAVORITE MEAL

BREAKFAST

LUNCH

DINNER

SNACKS

RELIGION

FAVORITE BOOK(S)/SONG(S)

Capture the Moments

Add photos or draw pictures that represent this chapter of your life.

Memories

Memories

"LIKE BRANCHES ON A TREE, WE ALL GROW IN DIFFERENT DIRECTIONS, YET OUR ROOTS REMAIN AS ONE."
— ANONYMOUS

A SPOUSE'S MEMOIR OF LOVE & DEVOTION

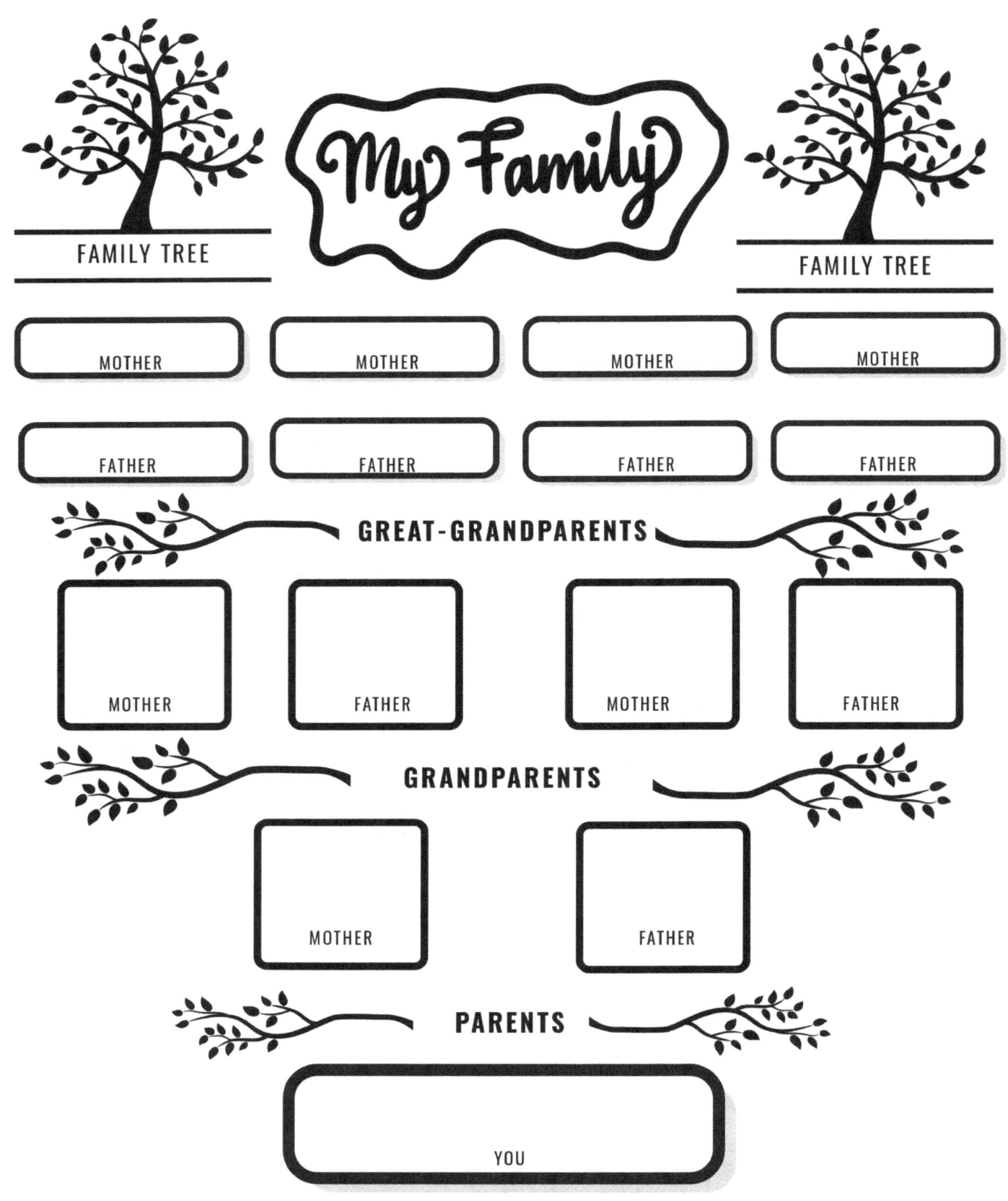

FAMILY TREE

My Family

FAMILY TREE

MOTHER

MOTHER

MOTHER

MOTHER

FATHER

FATHER

FATHER

FATHER

GREAT-GRANDPARENTS

MOTHER

FATHER

MOTHER

FATHER

GRANDPARENTS

MOTHER

FATHER

PARENTS

YOU

A SPOUSE'S MEMOIR OF LOVE & DEVOTION

Capture the Moments

Add photos or draw pictures that represent this chapter of your life.

Memories

Memories

> "THE STORIES WE LIVE BECOME THE STORIES WE LEAVE BEHIND."
> — ANONYMOUS

A SPOUSE'S MEMOIR OF LOVE & DEVOTION

OUR ORIGIN STORY

A SPOUSE'S MEMOIR OF LOVE & DEVOTION

HOW DID YOU MEET YOUR SPOUSE?

_____

_____

_____

_____

_____

_____

_____

_____

WHAT ARE THE LITTLE DETAILS YOU
NEVER WANT TO FORGET?

_____

_____

_____

_____

_____

_____

_____

_____

_____

WHAT FIRST DREW YOU TO EACH OTHER?

DESCRIBE YOUR FIRST REAL CONVERSATION— WHAT MADE IT MEMORABLE?

WHEN DID YOU KNOW THIS RELATIONSHIP WAS DIFFERENT?

_____

_____

_____

_____

_____

_____

_____

_____

WHAT PROMISE DID YOU MAKE EARLY ON THAT STILL MATTERS?

_____

_____

_____

_____

_____

_____

_____

_____

WHAT WAS YOUR FIRST CHALLENGE
AS A COUPLE, AND HOW DID YOU NAVIGATE IT?

_____

_____

_____

_____

_____

_____

_____

_____

_____

_____

_____

_____

_____

_____

_____

_____

_____

_____

WHO SUPPORTED YOUR RELATIONSHIP EARLY ON?

_____

_____

_____

_____

_____

_____

_____

_____

HOW?

_____

_____

_____

_____

_____

_____

_____

_____

_____

WHAT SYMBOLS, OBJECTS, OR PLACES MARK THE BEGINNING OF YOUR LOVE STORY?

WHAT ALMOST DIDN'T HAPPEN— BUT YOU'RE GLAD IT DID?

WHAT SONG, MOVIE, OR BOOK REMINDS YOU OF YOUR BEGINNING?

additional notes

additional notes

Capture the Moments

Add photos or draw pictures that represent this chapter of your life.

Memories

Memories

Memories

"WE DO NOT REMEMBER DAYS, WE
REMEMBER MOMENTS."
— CESARE PAVESE

A SPOUSE'S MEMOIR OF LOVE & DEVOTION

COURTSHIP & EARLY DAYS

A SPOUSE'S MEMOIR OF LOVE & DEVOTION

WHAT WAS YOUR FAVORITE DATE?

_____

_____

_____

_____

_____

_____

_____

_____

WHY?

_____

_____

_____

_____

_____

_____

_____

_____

_____

WHAT DID YOU LEARN ABOUT YOURSELF IN THE EARLY DAYS TOGETHER?

_____

_____

_____

_____

_____

_____

_____

HOW DID YOU CELEBRATE SMALL MILESTONES AS A COUPLE?

_____

_____

_____

_____

_____

_____

_____

_____

WHAT'S A PLAYFUL RITUAL OR INSIDE JOKE?

WHEN DID YOU FIRST MEET EACH OTHER'S FAMILIES?

_____

_____

_____

_____

_____

_____

_____

_____

HOW DID IT GO?

_____

_____

_____

_____

_____

_____

_____

_____

WHAT WAS A FAVORITE 'FIRST' —FIRST SMILE, WORD, STEP, OR DAY OF SCHOOL?

WHAT BOUNDARIES OR AGREEMENTS HELPED YOUR RELATIONSHIP GROW HEALTHY ROOTS?

DESCRIBE A TIME YOU CHOSE
EACH OTHER OVER CONVENIENCE.

_____

_____

_____

_____

_____

_____

_____

HOW DID YOU NAVIGATE DIFFERENCES
IN HABITS OR PREFERENCES?

_____

_____

_____

_____

_____

_____

_____

_____

_____

WHAT ADVENTURE DID YOU TAKE TOGETHER THAT BROUGHT YOU CLOSER?

_____

_____

_____

_____

_____

_____

_____

_____

_____

_____

_____

_____

_____

_____

_____

_____

_____

_____

WHAT ADVICE WOULD YOU GIVE YOUR YOUNGER SELVES AS A COUPLE?

_____

_____

_____

_____

_____

_____

_____

_____

_____

_____

_____

_____

_____

_____

_____

_____

_____

_____

additional notes

additional notes

Capture the Moments

Add photos or draw pictures that represent this chapter of your life.

Memories

Memories

Memories

"IN EVERY CONCEIVABLE MANNER, THE FAMILY IS THE LINK TO OUR PAST, BRIDGE TO OUR FUTURE."
— ALEX HALEY

A SPOUSE'S MEMOIR OF LOVE & DEVOTION

MARRIAGE & COMMITMENT

A SPOUSE'S MEMOIR OF LOVE & DEVOTION

TELL THE STORY OF YOUR PROPOSAL OR THE MOMENT YOU DECIDED TO COMMIT.

DESCRIBE YOUR WEDDING OR COMMITMENT CEREMONY

_____

_____

_____

_____

_____

_____

_____

_____

WHAT MOMENTS STAND OUT?

_____

_____

_____

_____

_____

_____

_____

_____

WHAT VOWS OR PROMISES GUIDE YOUR PARTNERSHIP TODAY?

_____

_____

_____

_____

_____

_____

_____

HOW DO YOU KEEP YOUR COMMITMENT ALIVE DURING ORDINARY WEEKS?

_____

_____

_____

_____

_____

_____

_____

_____

WHAT FINANCIAL, SPIRITUAL, OR PRACTICAL PRACTICES SUPPORT YOUR UNION?

HOW DO YOU HANDLE DECISION-MAKING AS A TEAM?

_____

_____

_____

_____

_____

_____

_____

_____

WHAT DOES PARTNERSHIP MEAN TO YOU
NOW VERSUS THEN?

_____

_____

_____

_____

_____

_____

_____

_____

_____

_____

HOW DO YOU REPAIR AFTER CONFLICT AND EXTEND GRACE?

WHAT DOES TRUST LOOK LIKE IN YOUR MARRIAGE?

HOW DO YOU CELEBRATE ANNIVERSARIES OR MARKERS OF TIME TOGETHER?

additional notes

additional notes

Capture the Moments

Add photos or draw pictures that represent this chapter of your life.

Memories

Memories

"WE ARE SHAPED AND FASHIONED BY WHAT WE LOVE."
— JOHANN WOLFGANG VON GOETHE

A SPOUSE'S MEMOIR OF LOVE & DEVOTION

DAILY LIFE TOGETHER

A SPOUSE'S MEMOIR OF LOVE & DEVOTION

WHAT DOES A TYPICAL WEEKDAY LOOK LIKE FOR THE TWO OF YOU?

_____

_____

_____

_____

_____

_____

_____

_____

WHAT SMALL HABITS MAKE YOU FEEL LOVED AND SEEN?

_____

_____

_____

_____

_____

_____

_____

_____

_____

HOW DO YOU DIVIDE HOUSEHOLD RESPONSIBILITIES— AND HOW HAS THAT CHANGED?

DESCRIBE YOUR FAVORITE WEEKNIGHT ROUTINE

_____

_____

_____

_____

_____

_____

_____

_____

WHAT IS YOUR FAVORITE WAY TO SPEND
A QUIET SATURDAY TOGETHER?

_____

_____

_____

_____

_____

_____

_____

_____

_____

HOW DO YOU PROTECT TIME FOR CONVERSATION AND FUN?

_____

_____

_____

_____

_____

_____

_____

_____

WHAT'S A SMALL ACT OF KINDNESS YOUR SPOUSE DOES THAT MATTERS A LOT?

_____

_____

_____

_____

_____

_____

_____

_____

HOW DO YOU NAVIGATE BUSYNESS
AND STRESS AS A TEAM?

_____

_____

_____

_____

_____

_____

_____

WHAT ORDINARY MOMENT
RECENTLY FELT EXTRAORDINARY?

_____

_____

_____

_____

_____

_____

_____

WHAT CUES HELP YOU NOTICE
WHEN THE OTHER NEEDS SUPPORT?

additional notes

69

additional notes

Capture the Moments

Add photos or draw pictures that represent this chapter of your life.

Memories

Memories

"IT IS NOT LENGTH OF LIFE, BUT DEPTH OF LIFE."
— RALPH WALDO EMERSON

A SPOUSE'S MEMOIR OF LOVE & DEVOTION

LOVE, JOY & HUMOR

A SPOUSE'S MEMOIR OF LOVE & DEVOTION

WHAT MAKES YOU LAUGH TOGETHER
UNTIL YOU CRY?

WHAT ARE YOUR FAVORITE 'JUST BECAUSE' GESTURES OF LOVE?

_____

_____

_____

_____

_____

_____

_____

_____

WHAT MOMENTS STILL GIVE YOU BUTTERFLIES?

_____

_____

_____

_____

_____

_____

_____

_____

_____

WHAT MUSIC, SHOWS, OR HOBBIES
DO YOU ENJOY TOGETHER?

_____

_____

_____

_____

_____

_____

_____

_____

HOW DO YOU KEEP PLAYFULNESS ALIVE?

_____

_____

_____

_____

_____

_____

_____

_____

WHAT'S A STORY YOU LOVE TO RETELL BECAUSE IT CAPTURES YOUR CHEMISTRY?

WHAT IS A COZY RITUAL THAT ALWAYS BRINGS YOU BACK TO EACH OTHER?

_____

_____

_____

_____

_____

_____

_____

WHAT COMPLIMENTS DO YOU TREASURE FROM YOUR SPOUSE?

_____

_____

_____

_____

_____

_____

_____

_____

DESCRIBE A SURPRISE ONE OF YOU PLANNED THAT WENT WONDERFULLY (OR HILARIOUSLY) WRONG.

WHAT ARE THREE THINGS YOU ADORE
ABOUT YOUR SPOUSE RIGHT NOW?

additional notes

additional notes

_____

_____

_____

_____

_____

_____

_____

_____

_____

_____

_____

_____

_____

_____

_____

_____

_____

_____

_____

_____

_____

_____

_____

_____

_____

_____

Capture the Moments

Add photos or draw pictures that represent this chapter of your life.

Memories

Memories

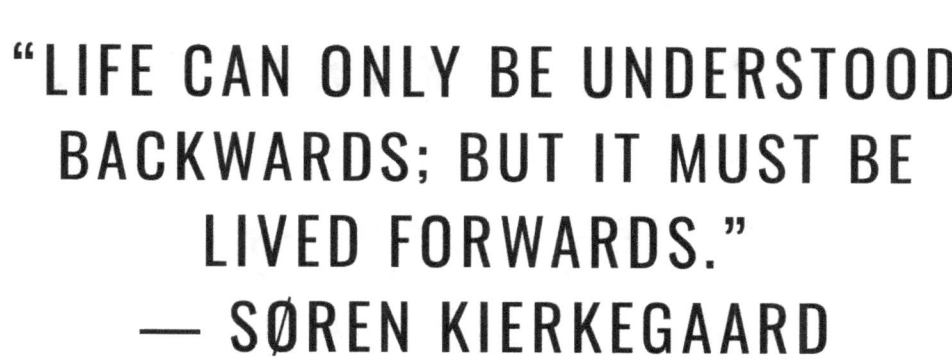

"LIFE CAN ONLY BE UNDERSTOOD BACKWARDS; BUT IT MUST BE LIVED FORWARDS."
— SØREN KIERKEGAARD

A SPOUSE'S MEMOIR OF LOVE & DEVOTION

CHALLENGES & GROWTH

A SPOUSE'S MEMOIR OF LOVE & DEVOTION

WHAT WAS A HARD MILESTONE THAT YOU GREW THROUGH TOGETHER?

WHAT BOUNDARIES PROTECT YOUR MARRIAGE?

HOW DO YOU HANDLE DISAGREEMENTS
ABOUT MONEY, FAMILY, OR TIME?

WHAT DOES APOLOGY AND REPAIR LOOK LIKE FOR YOU TWO?

_____

_____

_____

_____

_____

_____

_____

_____

WHEN HAVE YOU CHANGED BECAUSE OF YOUR SPOUSE'S LOVING CHALLENGE?

_____

_____

_____

_____

_____

_____

_____

_____

WHAT TOOLS (COUNSELING, MENTORS, BOOKS) HAVE STRENGTHENED YOUR MARRIAGE?

_____

_____

_____

_____

_____

_____

_____

_____

HOW DO YOU CARE FOR THE RELATIONSHIP DURING ILLNESS, GRIEF, OR SETBACKS?

_____

_____

_____

_____

_____

_____

_____

_____

_____

WHEN DID YOU CHOOSE TO START AGAIN—
WHAT DID RENEWAL LOOK LIKE?

_____

_____

_____

_____

_____

_____

_____

_____

_____

_____

_____

_____

_____

_____

_____

_____

_____

_____

HOW DO YOU MAKE SPACE FOR BOTH INDEPENDENCE AND TOGETHERNESS?

WHY IS IT IMPORTANT?

WHAT DID YOU LET GO OF TO MAKE ROOM FOR SOMETHING BETTER TOGETHER?

additional notes

□ _____
  _____
  _____
  _____

_____
_____   □
_____
_____

□ _____
  _____
  _____
  _____

_____
_____   □
_____
_____

□ _____
  _____
  _____
  _____

_____
_____   □
_____
_____

□ _____
  _____
  _____
  _____

additional notes

Capture the Moments

Add photos or draw pictures that represent this chapter of your life.

Memories

Memories

Memories

"THE MEANING OF LIFE IS TO FIND YOUR GIFT. THE PURPOSE OF LIFE IS TO GIVE IT AWAY."
— PABLO PICASSO

A SPOUSE'S MEMOIR OF LOVE & DEVOTION

FAMILY & COMMUNITY

A SPOUSE'S MEMOIR OF LOVE & DEVOTION

HOW DO YOU STAY CONNECTED WITH EXTENDED FAMILY AND FRIENDS AS A COUPLE?

WHAT ROLE DO TRADITIONS AND GATHERINGS PLAY IN YOUR LIFE TOGETHER?

WHAT CAUSES, FAITH COMMUNITIES, OR GROUPS DO YOU SERVE TOGETHER?

HOW DO YOU SHOW HOSPITALITY—WHAT DOES 'WELCOME' LOOK LIKE IN YOUR HOME?

HOW DO YOU SUPPORT EACH OTHER'S RELATIONSHIPS BEYOND THE MARRIAGE?

WHAT DOES IT LOOK LIKE TO BE A TEAM IN PARENTING OR CAREGIVING?

WHAT BOUNDARIES HELP WITH IN-LAWS AND EXTENDED FAMILY DYNAMICS?

_____

_____

_____

_____

_____

_____

_____

HOW DO YOU CELEBRATE OTHERS' MILESTONES AS A PAIR?

_____

_____

_____

_____

_____

_____

_____

_____

WHEN HAVE YOU LEANED ON YOUR COMMUNITY, AND WHO SHOWED UP?

_____

_____

_____

_____

_____

_____

_____

HOW DO YOU PRACTICE GRATITUDE FOR THE PEOPLE AROUND YOU?

_____

_____

_____

_____

_____

_____

_____

_____

_____

additional notes

additional notes

Capture the Moments

Add photos or draw pictures that represent this chapter of your life.

Memories

Memories

"THE GREATEST USE OF LIFE IS TO SPEND IT FOR SOMETHING THAT WILL OUTLAST IT."
— WILLIAM JAMES

A SPOUSE'S MEMOIR OF LOVE & DEVOTION

HOME & SHARED SPACES

A SPOUSE'S MEMOIR OF LOVE & DEVOTION

DESCRIBE THE FIRST HOME YOU MADE TOGETHER?

WHAT MADE IT YOURS?

WHAT OBJECTS IN YOUR HOME TELL YOUR STORY?

HOW DO YOUR STYLES SHOW UP IN YOUR SPACE?

_____

_____

_____

_____

_____

_____

_____

_____

WHAT'S YOUR FAVORITE CORNER OR
ROOM AND WHY?

_____

_____

_____

_____

_____

_____

_____

_____

HOW DO YOU CREATE A SENSE OF PEACE AND REST AT HOME?

WHAT ROUTINES KEEP YOUR SPACE (MOSTLY) IN ORDER?

_____

_____

_____

_____

_____

_____

_____

_____

WHY?

_____

_____

_____

_____

_____

_____

_____

_____

HOW DO YOU HOST GUESTS—
WHAT FEELS MOST LIKE THE TWO OF YOU?

WHAT IS A MEAL YOU LOVE COOKING OR ORDERING IN TOGETHER?

WHAT DOES YOUR DREAM HOME OR RETREAT LOOK AND FEEL LIKE?

WHAT SCENTS, SOUNDS, OR TEXTURES DEFINE 'HOME' TO YOU BOTH?

additional notes

additional notes

Capture the Moments

Add photos or draw pictures that represent this chapter of your life.

Memories

Memories

> "THE GREATEST THING YOU'LL EVER LEARN IS JUST TO LOVE AND BE LOVED IN RETURN."
> — EDEN AHBEZ

A SPOUSE'S MEMOIR OF LOVE & DEVOTION

TRADITIONS, RITUALS & TRAVEL

A SPOUSE'S MEMOIR OF LOVE & DEVOTION

WHAT YEARLY OR SEASONAL TRADITIONS DO YOU LOVE MOST?

_____

_____

_____

_____

_____

_____

_____

WHAT IS A DATE-NIGHT RITUAL YOU PROTECT?

_____

_____

_____

_____

_____

_____

_____

_____

DESCRIBE A TRIP THAT CHANGED YOUR RELATIONSHIP—HOW SO?

WHAT TRAVEL TRADITIONS DO YOU HAVE (PHOTOS, JOURNALS, PLAYLISTS)?

_____

_____

_____

_____

_____

_____

_____

HOW DO YOU CHOOSE DESTINATIONS AND PLAN ADVENTURES?

_____

_____

_____

_____

_____

_____

_____

_____

WHAT IS A PLACE YOU RETURN TO AGAIN AND AGAIN—WHY?

WHAT IS YOUR FAVORITE MEMORY
FROM TRAVELING TOGETHER?

WHAT'S A TRAVEL MISHAP THAT TURNED INTO A GREAT STORY?

WHAT DESTINATION IS STILL ON YOUR SHARED LIST —AND WHY THAT ONE?

HOW DO YOU BRING THE FEELING
OF TRAVEL BACK HOME?

additional notes

additional notes

Capture the Moments

Add photos or draw pictures that represent this chapter of your life.

Memories

Memories

"OUR MOST TREASURED FAMILY HEIRLOOMS ARE OUR SWEET FAMILY MEMORIES."
— ANON

A SPOUSE'S MEMOIR OF LOVE & DEVOTION

LEGACY & DREAMS TOGETHER

A SPOUSE'S MEMOIR OF LOVE & DEVOTION

WHAT KIND OF MARRIAGE DO YOU WANT TO BE KNOWN FOR?

WHAT ARE YOUR SHARED HOPES FOR THE NEXT YEAR? FIVE YEARS?

HOW DO YOU WANT TO IMPACT
YOUR COMMUNITY TOGETHER?

WHAT PROJECTS OR CAUSES DO YOU DREAM OF BUILDING AS A TEAM?

WHAT STORIES FROM YOUR LOVE DO YOU WANT FUTURE GENERATIONS TO KNOW?

WHAT RITUALS OR LETTERS WOULD YOU LEAVE FOR ANNIVERSARIES TO COME?

HOW DO YOU PLAN FOR YOUR FUTURE—
FINANCES, HEALTH, AND FUN?

WHAT DOES GROWING OLD TOGETHER
LOOK LIKE IN YOUR IMAGINATION?

WHAT PROMISE DO YOU WANT TO RENEW TODAY?

WHAT BLESSING WOULD YOU WRITE FOR YOUR SPOUSE AND YOUR LIFE TOGETHER?

_____

_____

_____

_____

_____

_____

_____

_____

_____

_____

_____

_____

_____

_____

_____

_____

_____

additional notes

additional notes

Capture the Moments

Add photos or draw pictures that represent this chapter of your life.

Memories

Memories

"OWNING OUR STORY AND LOVING OURSELVES THROUGH THAT PROCESS IS THE BRAVEST THING WE'LL EVER DO."
— BRENÉ BROWN

A SPOUSE'S MEMOIR OF LOVE & DEVOTION

Life's *Reflections*

(Overview)
SUMMARIZE KEY EVENTS

(Achievements)
WHAT WERE YOUR MAJOR ACHIEVEMENTS?

(Gratitude)
LIST THREE THINGS YOU'RE MOST GRATEFUL FOR.

(Priorities)
IDENTIFY KEY PRIORITIES AND GOALS.

Dear LETTER TO LOVED ONE

_____ ,

_____

_____

_____

_____

_____

_____

_____

_____

_____

_____

_____

_____

_____

_____

_____

_____

_____

WITH LOVE,

_____

LETTER TO LOVED ONE

*D*EAR _____ ,

_____

_____

_____

_____

_____

_____

_____

_____

_____

_____

_____

_____

_____

_____

_____

_____

WITH LOVE,

_____

DEAR _____,

_____

_____

_____

_____

_____

_____

_____

_____

_____

_____

_____

_____

_____

_____

_____

_____

LETTER TO LOVED ONE

WITH LOVE,

_____

LETTER TO LOVED ONE

$\mathcal{D}$EAR _____ ,

_____

_____

_____

_____

_____

_____

_____

_____

_____

_____

_____

_____

_____

_____

_____

_____

_____

WITH LOVE,

_____

$\mathcal{D}$EAR LETTER TO LOVED ONE

_____ ,

_____

_____

_____

_____

_____

_____

_____

_____

_____

_____

_____

_____

_____

_____

_____

_____

_____

_____

_____

_____

WITH LOVE,

_____

Capture the Moments

Add photos or draw pictures that represent this chapter of your life.

Memories

Memories

Memories

Capture the Moments

Add photos or draw pictures that represent this chapter of your life.

Memories

Memories

"YOUR STORY IS WHAT YOU HAVE, WHAT YOU WILL ALWAYS HAVE. IT IS SOMETHING TO OWN."
— MICHELLE OBAMA

A SPOUSE'S MEMOIR OF LOVE & DEVOTION

ADDITIONAL
MEMOIR PUBLICATIONS

ROOTED IN YOU
A CHILD'S MEMOIR OF LOVE AND GRATITUDE

THE LIGHT THAT LINGERS
A PERSONAL MEMOIR OF LOVE AND LIFE

CARRIED IN MY HEART
A MOTHER'S MEMOIR OF LOVE AND LEGACY

GUIDED BY MY HANDS
A FATHER'S MEMOIR OF LOVE AND STRENGTH

AFOR MORE INFORMATION OR
TO PURCHASE ADDITIONAL COPIES
WWW.ATOSHALOGAN.COM

Every life tells a story...

Love, in its truest form, is a journey of partnership—weathering storms, celebrating milestones, and cherishing quiet moments in between. This memoir is a testament to the bond of two lives intertwined. With tenderness and truth, it honors the beauty of commitment, the strength of unity, and the lasting legacy of shared love.

More than a record of one life, this memoir is an invitation to reflect on your own story. It is a reminder that while we cannot choose every circumstance, we can choose the legacy we leave behind.

Whether you are seeking encouragement, reflection, or simply a heartfelt story, this book offers something to carry with you. May it inspire you to embrace your own journey with gratitude, courage, and love.

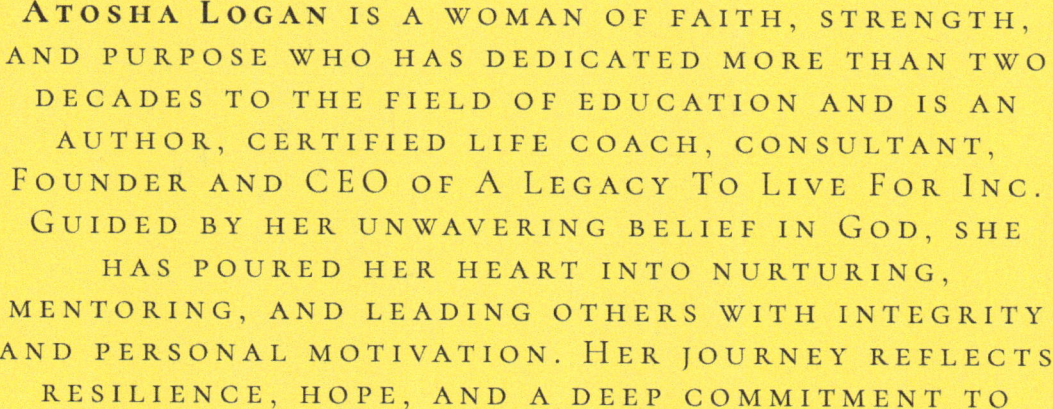

Atosha Logan

Atosha Logan is a woman of faith, strength, and purpose who has dedicated more than two decades to the field of education and is an author, certified life coach, consultant, Founder and CEO of A Legacy To Live For Inc. Guided by her unwavering belief in God, she has poured her heart into nurturing, mentoring, and leading others with integrity and personal motivation. Her journey reflects resilience, hope, and a deep commitment to uplifting and empowering others.